info buzz

Christianity

Izzi Howell

W
FRANKLIN WATTS
LONDON • SYDNEY

Franklin Watts

First published in Great Britain in 2018 by The Watts Publishing Group

Copyright © The Watts Publishing Group, 2018

Produced for Franklin Watts by
White-Thomson Publishing Ltd
www.wtpub.co.uk

ISBN: 978 1 4451 5962 1

10 9 8 7 6 5 4 3 2 1

Credits

Series Editor: Izzi Howell
Original concept: Rocket Design (East Anglia) Ltd
Designer: Clare Nicholas
Literacy consultant: Kate Ruttle

The publisher would like to thank the following for permission to reproduce their pictures: Getty: fotoMonkee 4, FatCamera7, 9l, 9r and 13, Digital Light Source/UIG via Getty Images 8, kokophoto 10l, Roberto Machado Noa/LightRocket via Getty Images 12, choja 14, isitsharp 15, Studio-Annika 16, Laures 19t, margouillatphotos 19b, Dmitry Chulov 20; Shutterstock: Gelpi cover, Nancy Bauer 5, Freedom Studio 6, Africa Studio 10r, AS photo studio 11 and title page, Monkey Business Images 17, Nattesha 18, mec17 21.

Every attempt has been made to clear copyright. Should there be any inadvertent omission please apply to the publisher for rectification.

Printed in China

Franklin Watts
An imprint of
Hachette Children's Group
Part of The Watts Publishing Gro
Carmelite House
50 Victoria Embankment
London EC4Y 0DZ

An Hachette UK Company
www.hachette.co.uk
www.franklinwatts.co.uk

All words in **bold** appear in the glossary on page 23.

Contents

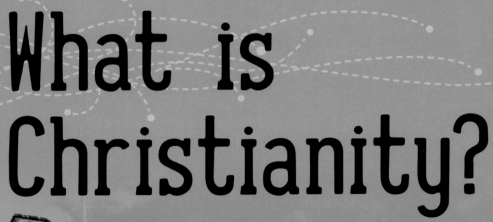

What is Christianity?

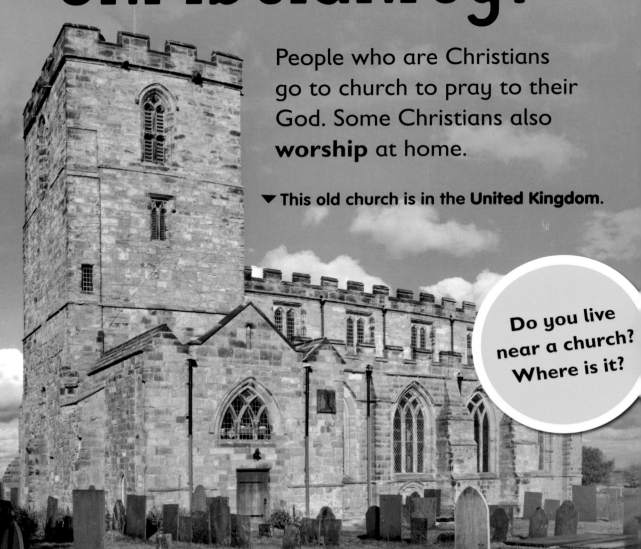

People who are Christians go to church to pray to their God. Some Christians also **worship** at home.

▼ This old church is in the **United Kingdom**.

Do you live near a church? Where is it?

Christians follow the ideas of Jesus Christ.
They think that Jesus was the son of God.
God sent Jesus to help people on Earth.

▲ This is a church window. It shows a picture of Jesus.

The Bible

Christians read the Bible.
The Bible is a book of stories
about God and Jesus.

▼ In one Bible story, Jesus helped
a blind man to see again.

Some Christian
families read
the Bible
together. ▶

The Bible has rules in it. The rules tell people how to be good Christians. Christians shouldn't lie or steal.

What are the rules at your house?

7

Going to church

Christians go to church on Sunday morning. They listen to a **priest** talking about Jesus and God.

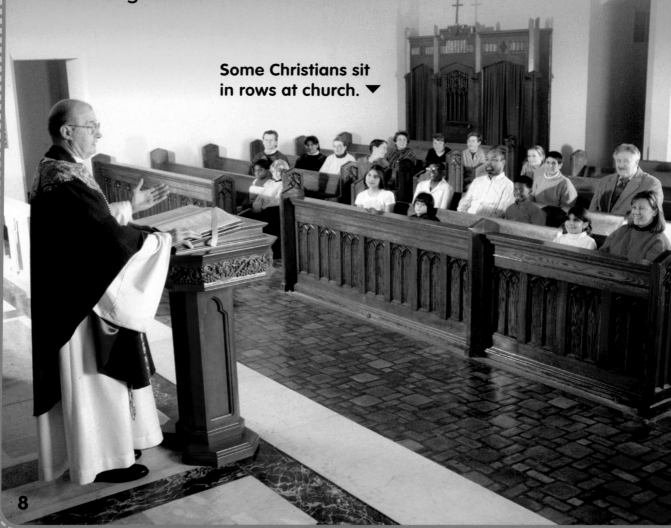

Some Christians sit in rows at church. ▼

Christians pray together at church. Sometimes, children go to Sunday school at church to learn more about God and Jesus.

What do you do on Sunday?

This girl is learning from her teacher at Sunday school. ▶

◀ At church, people sing Christian songs called hymns.

Communion

Some Christians share bread and wine at church. This is called **communion**.

wine

bread

◀ The priest says prayers about the bread and wine.

When do you share food? Who do you share it with?

Communion helps Christians to remember Jesus. Jesus ate bread and wine with his friends before he died. ▶

Christian children celebrate the first time they take communion. Girls wear white dresses and boys wear **suits**.

▼ Some children carry candles at their First Communion.

11

Praying

Praying is a way of talking to God. Christians thank God for good things. They ask God for help for themselves and other people.

◀ Some Christians kneel to pray in church.

Who do you ask for help?

Christians put their hands together to pray. When they have finished, they say 'amen'.

Some Christians pray before bedtime. Christians shut their eyes when they pray. ▶

A Christian life

Christians have different **celebrations** during their life. Babies are **baptised**.

▲ At a baptism, the priest pours water on the baby's head. Then he or she says the baby's name.

Some Christians get married when they are adults. They have a wedding in a church. When Christians die, they have a funeral in church.

The priest reads from the Bible at a wedding. Then the couple makes promises to look after each other. ▼

How do you think people feel at a funeral?

Christmas

Christians celebrate Christmas on 25 December. Christmas is about the birth of Jesus.

▲ These children are in a nativity play. They are acting out the story of Jesus' birth.

Christians go to church at Christmas. Then they have a big meal at home with their family and friends.

▼ People give each other presents at Christmas.

How does it feel to give a present?

Easter

At Easter, Christians remember the death of Jesus. Christians believe that Jesus came back to life after he died.

▲ Christians think that Jesus later went to **heaven**.

Easter happens in the spring. Christians celebrate by going to church. They also eat special food, such as Easter eggs.

paint

◀ Some Easter eggs are made from chocolate.

Around the world

There are many Christians around the world. Christians live on different **continents**, such as Africa, Asia and Europe.

These boys are Christians. They live in the country of Ethiopia in Africa. ▶

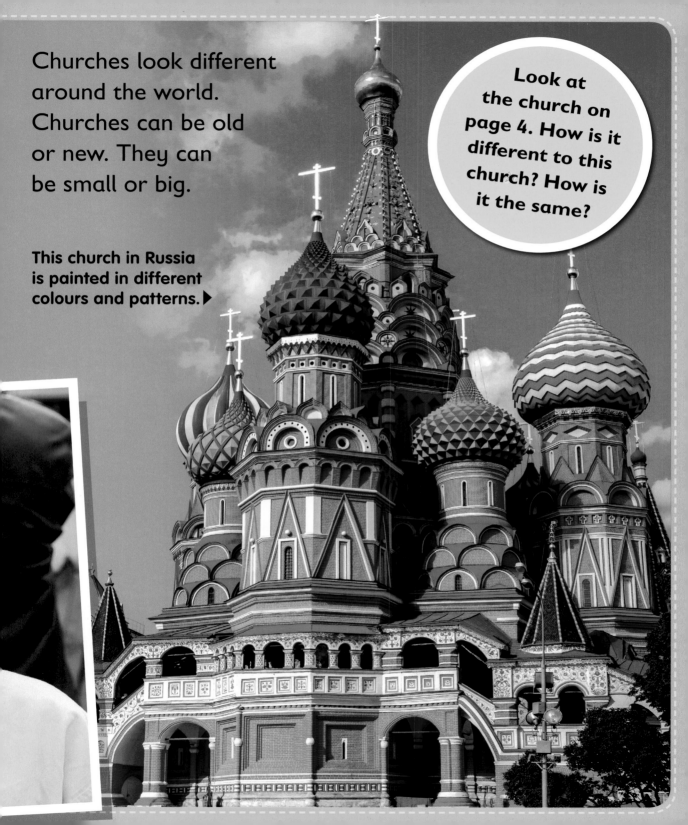

Churches look different around the world. Churches can be old or new. They can be small or big.

This church in Russia is painted in different colours and patterns. ▶

Look at the church on page 4. How is it different to this church? How is it the same?

Quiz

Test how much you remember.

Check your answers on page 24.

1 Who is Jesus?

2 What is a hymn?

3 What do Christians say after praying?

4 What happens at a baptism?

5 On which date is Christmas?

6 When do people remember the death of Jesus?

Glossary

baptised – given a Christian ceremony where water is poured on the body

celebration – a special day or event

communion – when Christians share bread and wine at church to remember Jesus

continent – a large area of land that is split into different countries

heaven – Christians think that good people go to heaven when they die

hymn – a Christian song

nativity play – a play that tells the story of the birth of Jesus

priest – a leader of a Christian church

suit – a set of clothes with trousers, a shirt and a jacket

United Kingdom – a country that includes England, Scotland, Wales and Northern Ireland

worship – pray or do something special to show that you think your god is important

23

Index

Answers:

1: The son of God; 2: A Christian song; 3: Amen; 4: A priest pours water on a baby's head and says the baby's name; 5: 25 December; 6: Easter

Teaching notes:

Children who are reading Bookband Gold or above should be able to enjoy this book with some independence. Other children will need more support.

Before you share the book:

- Are any of the children in your class Christians? Can they tell you about their experiences and understanding?

- Talk together about the religions of other children. What is the same/what is different from Christian children's experiences?

While you share the book:

- Help children to read some of the more unfamiliar words.

- Talk about the questions. Encourage children of different faiths to share their own answers.

- Talk about the pictures. Introduce some more technical language related to Christianity to describe what you can see in the pictures such as: steeple (p4), stained glass (p5), Old/New Testament (p6), parable (p6), pew (p8), font (p14), dome (p21).

After you have shared the book:

- Arrange to take the children to visit a church. Ask them to look for things mentioned or shown in the book.

- Share some Bible stories with the children. What can they learn about Jesus or about Christians from the Bible stories?

- Work through the free activity sheets from our Teacher Zone at www.hachettechildrens.co.uk.

Series Contents Lists

Religion

978 1 4451 5962 1

What is Christianity?
The Bible
Going to church
Communion
Praying
A Christian life
Christmas
Easter
Around the world

978 1 4451 5964 5

What is Hinduism?
Hindu books
The mandir
Worship
At home
A Hindu life
Divali
Holi
Around the world

978 1 4451 5968 3

What is Islam?
The Qur'an
The mosque
Praying
Clothes
A Muslim life
Ramadan
Eid al Fitr
Around the world

978 1 4451 5966 9

What is Judaism?
The Torah
The synagogue
Worship
Shabbat
A Jewish life
Hanukkah
Purim
Around the world

History

978 1 4451 5948 5

978 1 4451 5886 0

978 1 4451 5950 8

978 1 4451 5952 2

Countries

Argentina 978 1 4451 5958 4
India 978 1 4451 5960 7
Japan 978 1 4451 5956 0
The United Kingdom 978 1 4451 5954 6

FRANKLIN WATTS